DEAR CONTINUUM

LETTERS TO A POET CRAFTING LIBERATION

Also by Mariahadessa Ekere Tallie

Karma's Footsteps

Dear Continuum
Letters to a Poet Crafting Liberation

Mariahadessa Ekere Tallie

**GRAND
CONCOURSE
PRESS**

Published in the United States by:
Grand Concourse Press

ISBN-13: 978-0692430903
First Edition.

Book & Cover Design: Bonafide Rojas
Cover Art: Crystal Clarity "The Seed"
www.artthirsty.com

*Many thanks to the editors of the following publications
in which some of these letters appeared:*

Her Kind: "Letter One"
The Pierian: "Letter Two," and "Letter Five"
THIS: "Letter Twelve"
Estuary: "Letter Four," "Letter Eight," & "Letter Fourteen"
The Mom Egg: "Rebirth"
VIDA: Women In Literary Arts: "The World is Much Less Safe"

Grand Concourse Press
1791 Grand Concourse #4D
Bronx, NY 10453
www.grandconcoursepress.com

Dedicated to Margaret Rose Medellin
who saw this book in me before I did & to my very
own Continuum, tucked within, growing day by day.
Thanks for showing up right on time.
I love you.

Contents

Introduction   x

Letters   13

Essays   65

Notes   81

References   85

Gratitude   87

Introduction

It's a surprise to me that I've written this book. I've had it in mind to write letters to a new mother for some time, and I thought that was the book I was going to write; but one day I found myself in a fit and it had to do with writing. I was disillusioned by things I was seeing in the world of poetry, and so I wrote one letter in an inspired blaze hoping to let younger poets know about the journey they were about to take. I think I also needed to remind myself of the truths contained in that letter. I often say, "I wish someone had told me these things when I started."

The letter was published on *Her Kind*, a now defunct section of the VIDA: Women In Literary Arts website. Readers called it motivational and courageous; some said they too had experienced what I had shared. I went on writing poems, grading papers, and raising children. Then I had a speaking engagement at Texas A&M International University as the feature for the Voices in The Monte Series. I was to spend two hours talking about the craft of writing. Two hours! I wondered how I could spend so much time talking about craft without putting people to sleep. I decided to write another letter specifically about how I approached writing. When I arrived at TAMIU that letter was not complete. The recipient of it was nameless and I wasn't clear what else I had to say. It was less than 24 hours before my talk.

Kimberly Thomas, the Director of the TAMIU Writing Center, took me to meet her staff. As I stood in that welcoming space meeting the people who had helped make my visit happen, I noticed students lining up to my left. I assumed they needed to talk to Kimberly, but it turned out those students were lined up to meet *me*. Some of them had read my work, others had seen my cinepoems. I was stunned. I was humbled. I was grateful. Suddenly, it was very clear to me what I had to say about writing. I went to my room and wrote. I finished the second letter and immediately wrote a third. "Dear Continuum" the letters began, because I had looked in the eyes of those students and seen exactly whom I was writing for and to. Those students, whose faces were full of light, warmth, and love, were a continuum of my work just as I am a continuum of so many other people's work.

The next morning I did my talk and shared the three letters. This particular talk felt more like a family reunion than an academic address. The students asked many thoughtful questions about my writing and they were intrigued by Continuum. Then a young woman, Margaret, raised her hand and asked, "Are you planning to write more of these and publish them in a book?" I let her know that if I did do that, I'd dedicate the book to her.

When I read one of the letters at the University of Southern Mississippi, Cheryl Jenkins, one of my fabulous hosts, asked me what I thought Continuum looked like. "Is Continuum male or female?" My answer was, "either one" and it still is. If Continuum were a woman, I'd warn her about how she'd have to be prepared to call her poet brothers out on sexist behavior. I'd probably tell her that I used to only wear baggy clothes early in my career hoping to be taken seriously. I'd tell her that through my work with other women, I'd learned I didn't have to box myself into certain subject matter or restrict my clothing choices to be heard. I'd tell her that the same conditions we hope to transform in the world through our work exist within the world of writing.

I'd also tell her to write about anything she wants to: her body, her hair, sex, birth, abortion, orgasm, infertility, menopause, menstruation. I'd tell her to allow her reality to be the norm in her work and warn her away from any notion of craft that says she must cut herself off from her physical self.

If Continuum were male, I would encourage him to share his truths in his writing and not be afraid to put his soul on paper instead of building a persona through words. I'd tell Continuum that his poems, his discussions, his actions could spark dialogues about issues like rape, police brutality, the environment, or domestic violence. I'd stress to him the importance of being a courageous ally to women. I would encourage him to organize supportive, safe spaces with other men to talk about their own difficulties.

Being an artist is beautiful and it is hard. Envisioning peace in a country that is perpetually at war is a challenge. Moving my pen helps me maintain my faith in peace, love, and justice. Seeing younger artists dedicated to art and liberation inspires me to no end. If it were not for the Continuums of the world, I would have put away my pen a long time ago.

Mariahadessa Ekere Tallie
NYC 2015

Dear Continuum

One

Dear Continuum:

I got an issue of *Poets and Writers* in the mail yesterday. I enjoyed what I read, but it was not inspiring at all. It was realistic. It was honest about the uphill battle it is to get a book seen. I know the work of this all too well. But this letter is not about books, this is about voice and the love and armor you will need to have yours heard.

When I think about being a writer in 2015, being a writer with a Black woman's voice—as Lucille Clifton said, "I am a black woman poet...and I sound like one."—with no agent, no powerful mentor opening doors, no financial support, no salary, no benefits, then I realize that this really is a crazy path. Deciding to be a writer was beautiful. Writing is beautiful. Deciding that my concerns, dreams, hopes, and voice are valid, and committing myself to putting my visions on paper has been a deeply healing experience. This work connects me to people I have never set my eyes on. However, being a writer in a country that does not support art and writing from the heart of my Black woman mama mouth is a struggle that sometimes leaves me speechless. (But the point is to exhaust me/us beyond words, isn't it? So I rest up and speak on.) Beloved, this landscape is actually more treacherous now than when I started nineteen years ago. I don't say this to discourage you, I say this because you need to know that you are embarking on the path of most resistance; if you plan to walk it, you need to study and you need to endure.

Listen, there is all sort of color in academic conferences and departments now. Much of that writing is non-threatening and status quo. It's the type of work that could have come from 18ᵗʰ-century nowhere. It's work that no one in our communities or families could wrap around cold shoulders or grasp onto in desperate moments or even nod at in faint recognition. That, we are constantly being told, is poetry. That exsanguinated verse. But you and I both know poetry can be soulful, grounded, gravity-defying and irrepressible. If your poems walk picket lines, work in soup kitchens, gather dandelion leaves, sweat, jump rope, wear stilettos, shout, give birth, watch the phases of the moon, or know that it is appropriate to put flowers in the ocean on New Year's Eve and pour liquor on the earth before anyone living takes a sip, then supposedly they are not poems. Supposedly, you missed the memo on craft, and your poems will be returned to sender. Save your postage. Honor your time.

Tap your Cimarron blood, tap the defiant DNA that gives your hair such good posture. Find a community of poets dedicated to writing and walking and being liberation. Study Hughes, Baldwin, Walker, Hurston, Shange, Baraka, Hayden, Dumas, Bandele, Johnson, Girmay, Moore, Rux, Hammad, Clifton, Rich, Boyce-Taylor, Medina, Madhubuti, Brooks, Forche, Ya Salaam, Rojas, Rivera, Knight, Esteves, Kaliba, Simmons, Kaufman, Sanchez, Finney, Betts, Espada, & Perdomo. This is your work and there are so many more to study; you will find them as you make your way. Read, write, edit and find a way—let the poems find their way—get those words read and heard. Find someone unbought to publish your stuff. Be really brave and publish the work yourself, but don't stop there. Publish the poets around you who stand on the frontlines and refuse to bow down. Publish those mamas bringing their babies to readings, those poets whose works are in anthologies that they read in the food stamp office, those lettered poets who can't make the rent, those poets with a day job who organize free workshops and salons, those poets who never lose their accents, the ones cast off in a spoken word ghetto because they actually dare to connect with an audience. Publish all of them, who are all of us, who fight this fight because we are determined to keep the doors open for the next generation, and because we would go crazy without our tongues, without our pens braiding the strands of our thoughts into some type of beauty. Not pressing our voices flat. Flat to that white rageless whisper. Not doing that and paying a heavy price.

And so it is.

One,
Mariahadessa

Two

For the tale of how we suffer, and how we are delighted, and how we may triumph is never new, it always must be heard. There isn't any other tale to tell and it's the only light we've got in all this darkness.

-James Baldwin

Dear Continuum:

It was good to receive your letter. I'm glad you were able to use some of my advice on editing. Remember that I can give you suggestions, but you will soon start to find your own rhythm. You asked me so many thoughtful questions; I'll start with the one about what it means to be a writer.

I think being a writer means being a person. Being human. Humane. Being engaged. Being open. Curious. Caring. Being able to listen and look deeply. Being an artist means being connected with truth and speaking the truth as it reveals itself to you. Being an artist means that your heart will break, and it will be your work to mend it again and again.

You are right that my art is one form of my activism. This is because I have been the beneficiary of carefully chosen words delivered with love. Words delivered with love by Alex Haley and Malcolm X caused me to look in the mirror one day and stop frowning at my own face. I understood the history of my nose, mouth and skin and suddenly, I was proud. Can you imagine? Those same words helped me to revel in the thicket of my hair, stop being ashamed, and I understood then, in a way I had not before, the power of the word. This is called "Nommo" by the Dogon. I attempt to wield my words as wisely as I would any sharp tool. It's the job of the writer to do this.

Here is a story for you. A friend and I were talking about faith and natural healing. We were talking about the plants and prayer and our elders and all the wisdom they had that we needed to tap back into. My friend asked me if I'd ever heard of "talking the fire out." I said I hadn't. She went on to explain to me that her mother was able to use words—prayerful, intentional, words—to make a person's burn stop stinging and that was called "talking the fire out." Now this is not fiction. So I said, "wow" because what else do you say to something like that? I remembered wishing I had the ability to "talk the fire out" too, but now I realize that in a way, I do. I realize that many times when I put my pen to paper it is an attempt to write the fire out. It's an attempt to write the pain, the stinging out of some wound or another. So when I decided to be a writer I decided my work would serve this purpose. When my work is not celebrating something, it is bearing witness to pain and the process of the healing which is a celebration of another kind. This is the celebration of resilience and the writing is—no matter how painful the subject matter—a shout of joy at still being here.

Consider that when you create art, you have medicine in your hands. Consider that you can pull people together for just reasons. What is just? I'd say it is what does not oppress or dismiss the humanity of anyone. What is just is compassionate and of love. I mean real love, which is not always romantic or beautiful. I mean the type of love that wakes up at 4 a.m. to work and provide a better life for a family, the love we saw at marches during the '60s, real love that does laundry, brushes hair, tills the soil, plants trees, chains itself to pipelines. Hard love. Difficult conversations and the willingness to sit down at the table to have them. Our writing can be all of that: the conversation, the table and the willingness. When I talk about art and activism, I am talking about love.

And so, even with all of your pointed questions about editing, knowing when a poem is done, and what to do to become a better writer, I ask you to remember that the life you live is art. Sit with yourself and ask why you want to be a writer. Determine what purpose you want your words to serve in the world.

Please send me your answer.

One,
Mariahadessa

Three

Dear Continuum:

I'm so relieved you're feeling better, and I'm really glad you got to experience the healing powers of mullein and echinacea. When I started working with plants and flowers, it was as if everything around me took on new life. I couldn't even pass dandelions without smiling. Medicine just growing in the cracks of sidewalks. Medicine everywhere.

What is my writing process? I always want to run when someone asks that because I'm not a person with any hard and fast rules about how or when or where I write. I don't have any rules for you either. No one but you can truthfully gauge your dedication to your work and your craft. Following someone else's rules about when to write or how often seems counterintuitive when it is your voice you're trying to find. I don't have a lucky pen or a special desk (I don't even have a desk). I don't write at a particular time of day or night. I don't even need quiet to write a poem. What I need is mental space—that is, I need to tune out everything around me and tune into the words inside. In my case, the words don't come from prodding, pushing or demanding; they come from entering a space of surrender, a space of deep listening. Editing is where the struggle begins, but not at the outset. Not in the beginning. This is the way my poetry comes.

How about this for a confession? There are days where I don't write poetry. Days. Weeks even. My most consistent writing is in my journal. I recommend that each writer get a journal and write in it at least three days a week. I write about whatever I want in mine—it's a private space to explore my thoughts, feelings, and ideas. Sometimes poetry comes during the exploration, most times it doesn't. A lot of the time when I'm not writing, I'm editing.

Sometimes when I feel stuck in a poem I share the piece with a friend to get feedback, but most times I keep my work to myself. I let it sit for awhile and go back to it later with fresh eyes. I have been part of collectives where we shared work and critiqued each other. I enjoyed that energy! It was stimulating, nourishing, and comforting to be in a supportive group. But because I moved around quite a bit and stayed off the poetry scene for years, I learned how to work alone as well. At this point I'm fortunate to have poetry communities I can drift in and out of, and friends I can depend on for honest, solid feedback.

Tell me more about your writing practice and what you're reading and what music you're listening to. I need some new sounds around me, and I liked that last mix you sent me!

Be well!!!

One,
Mariahadessa

P.S.
Since you want to look into plants, check out John Lust's *The Herb Book* and Gail Faith Edwards' *Opening Our Wild Hearts To the Healing Herbs.*

Four

Dear Continuum:

It was so good to get your letter. I was laughing out loud on the subway when I read it. It's good to hear that you've met some folks who share your passion for words and justice. When I started reading poetry on stages in the '90s, I was surrounded by some of the fiercest, most nurturing writers you can imagine. They were generous with their time, praise, and encouragement and they were considerate about their critiques. There is an art to all that. Nommo again. These poets knew the power of their words, so they spoke them deliberately.

Back then, I had a mentor whose advice on writing boiled down to one word "READ." I was already a reader so that was no big deal to me. I read the work of writers whose reasons for putting pen to paper were similar to mine. I started an intense study of Harlem Renaissance writers. That led to my study of the Black Arts Movement, self-identified Womanist writers, Nuyorican poets, Beat poets, Basho, and Issa. I was amazed when I met people who called themselves poets, but then explained that they didn't read poetry because they did not want to be influenced by other people. Imagine that. I wouldn't see a doctor who hadn't studied medicine or a lawyer who didn't study law, so why would I pay mind to a poet who didn't study poetry?

Anyway, you asked me what I think differentiates a journal entry from poetry or creative writing. I can say that my poetry begins where the journal entry ends. I write in my journal to clear myself. Anything goes in a journal entry. Fragments, rants, victories, questions, the day's events. It doesn't matter. Writing in my journal is like showering after running a marathon or dipping into a cool river after working on a farm all day. It's like getting clutter out of my apartment. Once the clutter is gone, I can look around the place and see what is there. That is where the poetry starts.

Of course, you know this does not mean my poetry is neat or full of answers. It doesn't mean it is crisp or sanitized. I believe in poetry that rises from the heart, the womb, the body, the Spirit. I believe in poetry that is yours. I believe in pages steeped in your sound and your reason for raising your voice.

I edit my poetry rigorously because I need to make sure my meaning is clear. And no, I don't think about audience when I write. I really don't. If you worry about that you'll find yourself trapped. You'll be tailoring your message or style to try to please people and that won't be your art anymore, will it? You'll be like a marionette and some imagined person's reaction will be pulling your strings. Yes, I know I am asking a lot from you, but you say you want to be an artist.

Oh, and listen, please try to understand your parents' point of view. It's not so much that they don't want you to be an artist, it is that they want you to be alright in this world. They want to know that you will have food on your table and a roof over your head, and they don't see art as a viable way to make that happen. I can only paraphrase Haki Madhubuti on this: he says that as poet you may not earn a living but you will certainly earn a life. Go easy on your parents. And keep writing.

One,
Mariahadessa

Reading List One

These books should keep you occupied for some time. I go back to them all the time.

Miguel Algarín and Bob Holman, *Aloud: Voices from the Nuyorican Cafe*
James Baldwin, *The Fire Next Time*
Ras Baraka and Kevin Powell, *In the Tradition: An Anthology of Young Black Writers*
Lucille Clifton, *Blessing the Boats: New and Selected Poems, 1988-2000*
Florence Howe and Ellen Bass, *No More Masks! An Anthology of Poems by Women*
Langston Hughes *The Collected Poems of Langston Hughes*
Audre Lorde, *Sister Outsider: Essays and Speeches*
Willie Perdomo, *Where a Nickel Costs a Dime*
Sonia Sanchez, *Homegirls and Handgrenades*
Ntozake Shange, *Nappy Edges*

Five

Dear Continuum:

In the age of e-mail, there is something special about getting your handwritten letters. I've seen research that says that what happens in our bodies and brains when we write is very different than what happens when we type. I've experienced that many times. How do you get your poems down on the page? If you tend to go to the computer first, why not experiment and see what happens with a pen in your hand? I still write my poems in longhand. All of this to say that it was great to receive a letter written in your script.

My travels have been refreshing. I am meeting young people who are dedicated to being critical thinkers. These budding scholars and artists give me so much hope for the future, in part, because they want to be creators and not merely consumers. A young man sitting in the front row at my reading at Wright State University in Ohio asked me a beautiful question. He asked me when and how I got the courage to go onstage and share my work. I remembered then that courage was not the thing that moved me to step on any stage. In fact, the only reason I ever got up in front of an audience to read poetry was that Ira B. Jones, the publisher of a literary journal called *Eyeball*, told me that sharing my work in front of an audience was an essential part of being a poet. I was horrified when he told me this. I'd envisioned the writer's life as me tucked away writing and getting my books stocked on shelves in stores. The idea of reading my poetry to people was— and sometimes still is—terrifying to me.

When I was a young poet, literally trembling in front of my audiences, I'd remember the words of

Audre Lorde: "Your silence will not protect you." She also wrote, "Because the machine will try to grind you into dust anyway, whether or not we speak. We can sit in our corners mute forever while our sisters and our selves are wasted, while our children are distorted and destroyed, while our earth is poisoned; we can sit in our safe corners mute as bottles, and we will still be no less afraid."

Those words strengthened me every time I interacted with an audience, and I carry them now as I did then. Lorde's words are a reminder that this writing and speaking is part of the work that needs to be done whether or not I am afraid.

What I told the young man in the front row was that I don't consider myself courageous; I'm doing what I have to do. I speak because these words are necessary. Somewhere out there, a woman is being terrorized; a billy club is drawing blood; someone is being stopped on the street because s/he wears, supposedly, suspect skin; there is a community garden being bulldozed. I speak to keep the circle unbroken. I speak because my ancestors had stories that no one wrote down in books. I speak so that we won't be invisible.

When my voice is no longer necessary, I'll pack it away. What I want to say to you is that our work is not about us. It is not about our courage or our fear. It is not even about us individually. It is about us collectively. I want to say that we owe it to the people who came before us, and to those who will show up long after we're gone, to speak the truth as we know it. We owe it to them to get the beauty and the ugliness on the page. That is love. Fear disappears in the face of that.

One,
Mariahadessa

Six

Dear Continuum:

I wish you light, absolute light, while you grapple with the loss of your friend.

No, what you wrote does not sound crazy. It makes complete sense. How do you regain your balance after this senseless, sudden loss? I don't know. I don't know if we regain our balance as much as we learn to move in a changed reality. The work seems to be to keep our hearts open even in the vice grip of grief and shock.

What did I do? What did I do when people I loved died suddenly? What did I do when my friend was murdered? What did I do when another was found in an estuary suffering from hypothermia and died in the hospital unidentified for days? What did I do when my mentor died from cancer? What did I do? I cried, Continuum. I cried. A lot. I talked to friends. I taught my classes. I wrote. There were difficult months when I wasn't sure I believed in anything: not justice, not Divine Order, not good over evil—none of that. My inner world was thrown into chaos. No. You don't sound crazy at all.

And what can poetry do for you now, you ask, and will there be a future? After those deaths, I didn't know whether the killer would be caught, I didn't know whether my friends went in peace. I didn't know what unlived dreams they took with them. I only knew one thing: one day I'd go where they had gone. Their deaths made me see that in a way I hadn't before. But those friends had lives we could celebrate. We told stories and laughed and cried and laughed again. They'd left us some beauty, and that's why we were devastated.

They'd shared something precious with us. So the only thing I could do—I realized—was live, and grieving was part of the living as surely as death would be.

Continuum, it's sometimes hard to think of poetry itself at a time like this. Our tears are commas. Every day we wake up, we are living stanza and verse. If words come, then let them and know they will be powerful. If words don't come, then just live. Just live and in time they will.

One,
Mariahadessa

Seven

Dear Continuum:

I hope all is well and this letter finds you in great health and spirits. I've been moving around quite a bit, and when I'm home, it's amazing how much work there is to do. I'm glad that summer is on its way and I can spend time with my daughters, read books, and start working with the earth again. I'm ecstatic when I don't have to set my alarm clock and every moment is not packed with something to do. The earth goes through seasons, the moon has phases, everything that is part of nature needs rest. I feel no guilt when I rest, and I hope you don't either.

Yes, becoming a mother did affect my writing. Profoundly. Mostly because motherhood affected my life profoundly, and much of my writing reflects my life. I think it is useful to be who we are. I mean really be who we are and write about the journey of that. I know the writers whose works strengthen me the most are the ones dedicated to speaking and writing their truths, even if those truths are complicated, uncomfortable, or unpopular. Think Audre Lorde, Chrystos, Essex Hemphill, or June Jordan.

When I became a mother, I made the decision that I would write about mothering. I knew I might lose the folks who paid attention to my poetry and my travel pieces, but I was willing to let that happen in order to write the truth I was living at that point. I met an entirely new community through that sharing. During that time I wrote when I could. That meant mostly when the baby slept, but there was a period when I didn't write at all. I had taken on another identity, and I needed time to get comfortable with it.

As soon as I felt somewhat at home as a mother, I started teaching again and thinking about the book of poetry waiting for me to start editing it. Then I found out I was expecting another baby. I was beyond thrilled. Writing fell to the wayside. I was engrossed in so many things and once the baby came, I was exhausted all the time.

When the urge to write resurfaced again my youngest daughter was one and her big sister was three. I wrote a booklet on self-care for new mothers and pregnant women. I also wrote a short essay called "Rebirth" that I'm including for you. It deals with some of the unspoken things many mothers go through.

Then, somehow, my friend, Cheryl Boyce-Taylor, called me back to poetry. She invited me to do the April 30/30 challenge that required that I write a poem every day of the month and share it with a small group. I did that, and I was amazed that I could. Then Cheryl asked me to participate in a poetry reading slated (appropriately) for Mother's Day. It was May 10, 2009. My husband and I took our three-and-a-half-year-old and almost two-year-old daughters to the reading. I met Marjorie Tesser, who publishes *The Mom Egg Review*, and I saw that there was a space for poet Mamas. We were gathered to break the bread of words, and I was glad I didn't have to leave any parts of myself behind that afternoon to share my poetry. I often say that with this reading, Cheryl brought me out of early retirement.

Soon after that reading I was an invited panelist at a conference on mothering. It was wonderful to bring my entire self to a space that was creative, academic, and dedicated to the work of mothers. I recommend that you take your whole self to the page when you write, and share your entire self with those gathered as your audience. Take your whole self, your broken self, your dancing self, your tired self, your fighting self, your sensual self, your contradictions and your integrity, your revelations and your missteps, your anger, your legs, your arms, your lips. See what I am saying? Be willing to even share your struggle to take your real self to the page.

I wandered back into poetry—or allowed it to wander back into me—by remaining open on my path as a writer. Allow yourself to write your truths without restrictions. Give yourself space and allow yourself to be changed.

One,
Mariahadessa

P.S.
My goodness, Continuum. I wish I did have a literary agent sending my work out, but they pretty much avoid poets unless we write fiction or non-fiction as well. I don't know any poets with literary agents. I hate to tell you that, but it's true. Look at it this way, though, we wouldn't be doing this work if we weren't up to the challenge. Our work will go where it needs to.

Eight

Dear Continuum:

I hope all is well. As you can see by the postcard, I am in Bahia. This is a sojourn I've wanted to make for well over a decade. Touching this soil feels like a reunion. I brought your letter here with me. The urgency in your questions made me do that.

Writing feels urgent, and it is urgent, but this idea of getting it "right" creates a pressure that does not seem to serve. What does it mean to get it right? Right according to who?

I experience the process of writing in many different ways. Sometimes it is like channeling. Other times it's a rite of passage. Often, writing is a conversation between the poem and me. Between me and me. Between the events of the world and my responses to them. Between people I love and me. When is a poem finished? I know a poem is finished much like I know a good conversation is over. I find myself sitting comfortably in silence. Everything that needed saying has been said. My words are like windows wiped down with distilled vinegar—my meaning is clear.

Sometimes, truths I don't consciously know reveal themselves during the writing process; I have got to be open to those truths. Again, it's like being in conversation, I have to hear everything being said to me, and I can't plan another person's words so I have to listen. When I am writing sometimes everything stops. It's as though I'm being handed words. When they land in my palm I sift through them carefully. I turn the words over and over. Study them as intently as I would a potential lover's eyes. It's a delicate, powerful motion. These unnamed things within step tentatively into the light, and the words that I am given either become their names or wait until I wrestle something truer from the invisible.

For me, the end of the poem is signaled by internal silence. Then the sounds of the voices around me, my hunger, my thirst, or the rumble of the subway become audible again. Some poems end with an explosion, and some end with a whisper. But when a poem has done its job, it never ends. It stays with the reader or the listener long after the last line.

One,
Mariahadessa

Nine

Dear Continuum:

I barely know where to start with this letter, but I've got to start somewhere if your work is going to get the light we both think it deserves.

It's great that you share your work through readings. There's nothing like an audience to let you know if a poem has any resonance—particularly an emotional one. Readings are important because we want our work to move in a world beyond the literary one. And yet, if you also want to create space for yourself within the literary world, you need to be serious about publishing. Keep in mind that there are many ways to go about getting your words in print. Whether we are talking about an entire manuscript or individual poems, you have options. You can consider independent presses, publications run by people of color, publishing collectives, academic presses, or you could publish yourself and your friends. Over the course of your writing career you might do all of these. I have.

When I started writing I had never heard of a literary journal. Most people go their entire lives without picking one up—which probably makes you wonder why you should bother trying to get in one— but that is part of the professional life of being a writer. Filmmakers have their journals, as do doctors, engineers, herbalists, and dancers. I was not an English major, and I did not go through an academic program that taught me about literary journals, but my introduction to them came early on. Ira B. Jones sent me a list of Black literary journals with their addresses and phone numbers. It was the generosity of community that taught me how to be a writer. I'd look those journals up in the library at Tuskegee University, and later at Clark Atlanta University, to study them. When I graduated, I'd spend hours at St. Mark's Bookshop doing the same thing. For what? To see where my writing might fit. I suggest you do the same. You can read the bios of contemporary writers you admire and see where their work was published. If their work has themes or an aesthetic similar to yours, you might consider sending work to those journals.

Back when I started doing this, there were no online journals, but you obviously have that world to explore as well. Keep your eyes open for calls for submissions for poetry, essays, papers, and fiction. Some online groups like Neo-Griot (my favorite) and magazines like *Poets and Writers* feature those. It goes without saying that you should follow whatever the submission guidelines are. If you can't find them for some odd reason, write to the publication and find out what the guidelines are.

It has taken me time to realize (or maybe accept) that getting published in certain journals carries more weight than appearing in others. Remember that the literary world reflects the system we are living in. There are certain journals that literary agents, editors, the folks who compile *The Best of...* anthologies read, and there are others that they don't even know exist. This does not have anything to do with the quality of the journals; it mostly has to do with narrow ideas about where good work could appear. It also has to do with narrow ideas about who can produce good writing. It is up to you to determine whether you are going to consider how journals are ranked. It's always up to you to decide how to direct your literary life. You might use different tactics at different times. Are you interested in wielding power and becoming a decision maker? Are you an institution builder? Do you just want your work in print? Considering these questions can help you figure out how to approach getting published. I've published myself twice, been anthologized by big presses, and my first book of poetry was put out by an independent press. I can tell you no matter which route you go, if you want to sell books, you've got to hustle. You'll have to do the publicity, set up your own readings, even get the books in stores sometimes. Nothing glamorous about it. It is work. Connecting with readers is what I see as my reward.

Like I told you, publishing has always been important to me, but I'm interested in other ways to get literature to people. Performances are one way. I've also worked with dancers and painters to widen the scope of my work. Now I'm creating cinepoems and fusing music with poetry. It's beautiful to reach people through different mediums. Then the art becomes something else. Part of my vision is to create a body of work that takes on its own life. The work can move in the world without me, facilitate discussion and feeling and action. That's what I work for.

I'm telling you this so that you can know the literary playing field and make informed decisions about what positions to take. You might decide to change the game. You might feel like you are writing for our lives and so this metaphor of games and playing does not apply. Whatever you decide, I'm here. We're here, applauding your voice.

One,
Mariahadessa

Reading List Two

Thrilled you asked for another list. I'm sure you'll have a lot to say about these also. Enjoy!

asha bandele, *absence in the palms of my hands*
Sandra Cisneros, *Loose Woman: poems*
Pearl Cleage, *Deals With the Devil: And Other Reasons to Riot*
Nikky Finney, *Rice*
Robert Frost & Edward Connery Lathem, *The Poetry of Robert Frost: the Collected Poems*
Etheridge Knight, *The Essential Etheridge Knight*
Alfredo Matilla Rivas & Iván Silén, *The Puerto Rican Poets. Los Poetas Puertorriqueños*
Cherríe Moraga and Gloria Anzaldúa, *This Bridge Called My Back: Writings by Radical Women of Color*
Nizār Qabbānī, *On Entering the Sea: The Erotic and Other Poetry of Nizār Qabbānī*
Lamont B. Steptoe, *Mad Minute*

Ten

Dear Continuum:

I hope this letter finds you in great health and spirits. Today I was walking home with three bags of groceries after spending much of the day washing dishes, checking my daughters' homework and doing other things that hold no excitement, and I thought, suddenly, that you should know this. Maybe you already do know it, but as I walked down Jamaica Avenue carrying shrimp and oatmeal and broccoli and apples I thought, "I should share this with you because it's not the stuff that makes it on Facebook." The day in, day out routines we're all familiar with aren't part of the feed. Maybe we go to social media for something out of the ordinary—and it certainly is great to log on and read about friends' new publications and projects, and see pictures of folks looking fabulous on stages across the world. But what gets us to those experiences is what goes missing from most of our timelines: the anxiety before a reading, creating draft after draft of a poem, the long and deadening waits between publications, the sadness and guilt at having to miss your child's performance because of your touring schedule, the wondering where the rent will come from, the endless waits in clinics because they have a sliding scale and are willing to see uninsured people— these are not generally the things we put on social media. And yet just about every artist I know well has gone through some of this at some point or another.

One friend got tired of having holes in his shoes so he put his paintbrushes down, got himself a job teaching at a middle school, and never looked back. Others left their art for real estate, social work or law.

And who can blame them? Living in a constant lack of certainty is tough on the spirit. Many folks find ways to balance jobs (often in academia) and their writing careers, but balance might not be the most appropriate word—juggling is more like it. And no matter how we do it, there are those moments—I know I've had them —those moments when I'm tired of swimming against the tide and I want to give up. Those are the moments I don't post on Twitter. So when I was walking home with those grocery bags, I thought about what my writing life might look like to you. You see my name in a masthead or a table of contents. You see pictures of me reading poems, smiling, laughing, hugging other writers. But I share these things precisely because they are the fruits of not giving up. And my goodness, those other writers and I are holding each other so tightly because we have gone through this journey together and we are still here. We are smiling, because in spite of all the rejection, nervousness, loneliness and longing, we still carry joy and words and possibility in us. We are smiling because we can still smile, despite living in a space that barely acknowledges our humanity, let alone our art.

It is all the unseen weeks, months, and years of work that create what you see on social media and in the literary magazines. Those moments are definitely as magical as they seem, in part, because they are evidence of our survival. I mean that in every way possible. So when you see those pictures of us glowing, just remember the hidden hours that led to them. Here's hoping that your hidden hours bear fruit.

One,
Mariahadessa

Eleven

Dear Continuum:

You really have been navigating the poetry world, haven't you? I have seen your name in quite a few places lately. Better still, I read your poems in two of my favorite journals, and I am so proud of you!

Please let your work and your very clear vision of the healing capacity of your work guide your steps. I know it is hard to see factions in art—the space we go for wholeness. I can certainly relate to how painful it is to see divisions happening among poets of color.

How did I deal with this? Honestly, I was naive and lucky in that I didn't realize how deep those divisions could go among poets of color until well after my first book was published. That is largely because the people who ushered me into the world of poetry didn't waste time on those types of issues. They were too busy writing, organizing, teaching, traveling, and mentoring poets like me. They didn't worry about someone's credentials. If a writer was dedicated to liberation, that was all that mattered to them. Have you read *In The Tradition* yet? That book was a map to me as I wandered and searched out a place to call home in poetry. In my mind, all the poets in that book were a unit. Their academic, economic, and personal backgrounds were as varied as their subject matter and that, to me, was an accurate reflection of how diverse we are. It was—and is—heartbreaking to see writers drawing lines in the sand and closing doors on each other because this one didn't or did go to college or that one did or did not get the fellowship or that one is Northern or Southern or that one is more of a spoken word artist, or isn't.

I've always seen poetry as a pure space. Things shift when people start taking their poetry to "the market." Suddenly poetry goes from being medicine to currency. Suddenly a poem can gain a person the things (recognition, respect, sex, power) they felt they were lacking. Remember the world of poetry is not the soul of poetry.

When poetry becomes a business (or an elite club or a bid for integration), it can't help but mirror everyday life in this country. In fact, even without poetry being a business, it reflects the classism, racism, sexism, and heterosexism of the country in which we live. What you are seeing, at times, is the ugliness of this country in stanza and verse.

Your work, our work, is to be aware of these things but not become embittered by them or get sucked into them. Some of my work has been an attempt to bridge the gaps between these worlds of poets. I've been encouraged in that task by some and told it's a useless endeavor by others. I just know we could create powerful spaces for each other if we'd honor each other's voices instead of trying to drown each other out. Most of our work is to write our visions. Write truth. Write wholeness into being and share what we've learned from our journeys. Much of our work is to create space where others feel safe doing the same.

Again, I am so proud of you!

One,
Mariahadessa

Twelve

Dear Continuum:

Your letter came just when I needed it. I'm glad that you feel you get something useful from my letters, but I have to tell you that the hope I get from yours is vital. The work you are doing with the teen parents and the writing workshops you are holding at the prison sound inspired. It is true that these voices rarely come into the light, yet we're incomplete without them.

I saw a comic strip many years ago. It was a one panel drawing of a white man smelling roses. The words underneath it were "Poet at Work." I clipped that and kept it for a long time because it rang true and made me laugh. I have been known to linger in fragrant flowers, give hugs to hearty trees, stare at stars and get loud about the gorgeousness of a crescent moon. Being suspended in the moment, present and available to the beauty that surrounds us, is something I see as being the job of the poet. I kept that comic strip for years, because it spoke to that part of the poet's reality. And yet, if I could draw, I'd create another comic strip to go alongside it. There would be many panels. There would be a brown woman in them. In the first panel she'd be planting flowers on a block where there is nothing green. In the next panel she would be standing in a room of thirty students writing the words: "their," "there," and, "they're" on the chalkboard. In the third panel she might be in a soup kitchen, at a rally, or folding laundry. She might be cooking dinner or helping a child with homework in the fourth panel. In the last one, she'd be looking into her beloved's eyes. The caption underneath these panels would also read "Poet at Work."

Ntozake Shange writes, "Poetry is unavoidable connection." Audre Lorde says, "Poetry is not a luxury." Ruth Forman writes, "Poetry should ride the bus." In your case and mine, our poetry and the way we live are entwined. I see my muse in almost everyone I encounter. It's in everything. I don't disengage to write. For me, writing is one of the ultimate forms of engagement.

One,
Mariahadessa

Thirteen

Dear Continuum:

I hope this card finds you in great health and strong spirits. Yes, there has been a whole lot going on lately, and I'm glad to see it too! It's about time people went out into the streets to make their voices heard. It's way overdue.

What have I been doing? Maybe I have been feeling more than doing this time around. After this last incident, I sat quietly for days trying to figure out what to do. Not just with my body or my words, but what to do with my rage. The rage I felt was so big it startled me. Flattened me even. I knew I couldn't be as effective as I wanted to be in that state. So I sat quietly. I called friends. I went to see an art exhibit. I wrote "Black Lives Matter" in sidewalk chalk on the streets. You see, we've been in the streets before. I am not an old lady, but I've been protesting one thing or another since I was sixteen. My first protest was outside of a courtroom in Brooklyn, and since then I've been at marches to prevent invasions, end wars, demand an end to police brutality, stand in solidarity with the Zapatistas, and insist that the killers of our children, grandmothers, brothers and sisters and lovers at least be arrested for their crimes.

And so, initially, I stayed still because history seemed to be repeating itself, and I was wondering if being in the streets was going to achieve any goal whatsoever. I thought about apartheid and the petitions I'd signed, and the products I refused to use or buy because the companies were investing in South Africa and thereby supporting apartheid. I thought about things I had not seen—like the bus boycott in

45

Montgomery. I know pulling money out of the system is an extremely effective way to make a statement heard. I started studying the armed resistance in Mississippi. Members of my own family used arms to defend themselves against racists in the South when it was necessary, and I thought it was important to research how effective that strategy had been. But more than anything else, I thought about what art could do. And I saw what art could do. I was at a temporary loss for words but when I danced, I felt a lot better. When I sang, I felt a lot better. When I saw visual art, I felt a lot better. My friend Cheryl read me the poem "Power" by Audre Lorde and it helped dislodge something in me. But I was still thinking about my poetry. What could it do, really do, when twelve-year-olds are being shot down by police on playgrounds, and twenty-eight-year-olds are being killed "accidentally" in stairways, and children's bodies are being left in the streets and no one is being held accountable? What the hell use is a poem then? I finally came to this: while poetry may not win the battle, it can move people to understand why the battle is necessary. It can help people decide to get involved.

I read a poem about rape to an audience of college students recently. During the Q&A a young man said that he had sat through training on preventing sexual harassment and assault in the military, but it had not affected him the way the poem had. He also said a poem I'd shared about a particular incident in Mississippi illuminated the devastation of racism. He said no seminar or training had shown him these things the way that the poems had. That is the power of art. The other powerful thing about poetry is that it helps people to envision another world, a better one. That is a huge gift when you're in the midst of struggle or despair. Remember, music and poetry helped soothe and strengthen people who were on the front lines of struggles globally. Sometimes the poets and musicians *were* on the front lines.

A lot of people share their poetry when painful events unfold and that is understandable, but I think we have to be conscious of what we do with art that comes from tragedy. I like to use art strategically to raise awareness about an issue and move people to action. An action can be small like signing a petition or big like donating resources (time, money, skills) to organizations. In some cases having readings to raise money for the families of the victims might be useful. We can also organize ourselves as artists and work collectively to support groups we believe in. It's important to me that the work I do be in the hands of people who can use it in practical ways. I'm excited when poems are used to facilitate discussions, or trainings, or healing sessions. When it comes to doing this work, it's our job to know the difference between exploring tragedy in a useful way and exploiting it to bring attention to our own work and ourselves. These are some of the reasons I sat still and considered what I was going to do very carefully.

In the end, of course, I went out into the streets, and I signed online petitions, and I donated what I could where I could. I'll find a way to make what I write useful. And I know you will too. Make sure you take good care of yourself. If you want to keep doing the work, you have to be as healthy and as centered as you possibly can be. We need you for the long haul. Pa'lante.

One,
Mariahadessa

Fourteen

Dear Continuum:

Do I think suffering is a prerequisite for great artistry? No. I don't. What I think is that most people suffer at some point, the artist just dares to admit it. I think awareness, empathy, strong observation skills, and the ability to listen deeply are necessary tools for any artist. Wisdom coupled with the willingness to admit that you really don't know much of anything are also instruments that will help you shape your art.

Do you ever listen to the blues? If not, I recommend you dip your toes in the sounds of Big Mama Thornton, Bessie Smith, Ida Cox, Howling Wolf, Leadbelly, and Son House. In "Uses of the Blues" James Baldwin writes that "they contain the toughness that manages to make this experience articulate." The blues are a testimony to our survival, strength, beauty, ugliness, and humor. They are a map, and the mere singing of the blues is the key. To navigate this sometimes rocky terrain of life, we have to tell our stories.

In that same essay Baldwin writes, "You don't know what the river is like or what the ocean is like by standing on the shore. You can't know anything about life and suppose you can get through it clean." Let me know what you think this means.

Continuum, when life is everything that the movies told you it would be, write. When life threatens to shatter you and rip your illusions to shreds, write. When you are distracted by romance, write. When you are consumed by heartache, write. When you are rejoicing, grieving, questioning, certain, write.

Life itself will give you a chance to feel

everything. I've never set a fire to feel flames singe me.
I already know flames will come. So will water.

One,
Mariahadessa

Reading List Three

Another word feast!

Pierre Bennu, *Bullsh*t or Fertilizer: A Portable Pep Talk*
Margaret Busby, *Daughters of Africa: An International
Anthology of Words and Writings by Women of African Descent
from the Ancient Egyptian to the Present*
Toi Derricotte, *Tender*
Thomas Sayers Ellis, *Skin, Inc.: Identity Repair Poems*
Aracelis Girmay, *Teeth*
Vicente Huidobro, *Altazor*
Tyehimba Jess, *Leadbelly*
Jacqueline Johnson, *A Gathering of Mother Tongues: poems*
Tony Medina, Samiya A. Bashir, & Quraysh Ali
Lansana, *Role Call: A Generational Anthology of Social and
Political Black Art & Literature*
John Murillo, *Up Jump the Boogie: poems*
Eugene B. Redmond, *The Eye In The Ceiling: Selected
Poems*
Bonafide Rojas, *When The City Sleeps*
Carl Hancock Rux, *Pagan Operetta*
Sonia Sanchez, *I've Been a Woman: New and Selected Poems*

Fifteen

Dear Continuum:

    I hope this letter finds you in great health and spirits. I know very well the feeling you've described: wishing you had wide swaths of silence to write in, but we both know our lives are not built like that. It's a feat that we manage to be creative and productive. I am grateful for every poem that I write between the meals I cook, the shopping I do, the classes I teach, the homework I correct, and the bedtime stories I read. I remain thankful beyond measure that I was chosen to do this work and that I answered the call.

    You ask what it was like when I started performing poetry. It was like anything and everything was possible. It was like living a dream every day. There were talented people everywhere, and no one's hand felt closed. My New York creative circle felt like a big family. Back then, I could step off the G train at Fulton Street, head to the Brooklyn Moon Cafe, and before I'd even get there, I'd be hugging someone and talking about the last poetry reading or the one coming up. Back then, it was a given that at 10 p.m. on a Friday night, I'd be in a small, blazing hot room packed with my new tribe. We'd share our poems into the morning and snap our appreciation because the neighbor upstairs did not want to hear clapping at 1 a.m. I remember one night, we took our revelry out onto the street, and the neighbor threw a bucket of water down at us as a way to shut us up. Those were beautiful days. I used to call my best friend at 2 a.m. asking her to listen to whatever I'd just written. Yes, community was everywhere. Back then I'd say, "I want to grow up and be like asha bandele." I'd never seen anyone pour her heart into a poem and touch a crowd the way asha does. I used to listen to Tony Medina explain why my being a music journalist was "just doing public relations for big corporations that didn't need any help."

At some point, my women friends and I decided to start a collective. It was a quick but resolute decision we made at the Kokobar when I was the sole woman reading on a bill of at least six or seven poets. On the spot, Mirlande Jean-Gilles, Nefertite Nguvu, Marcia Jones and I decided to take our destinies into our own hands and organize our own events. We called our collective Words and Waistbeads to represent works that contained all aspects of womanhood. In our work, we would rail against injustice while refusing to put our sensuality in the closet. Our goal was to be our complete selves and support each other on that journey, much like we imagined the poets on Shameless Hussy Press did back in the day. Working with Mirlande, Nefertite, and Marcia was liberating. We were invited to perform at Rutgers University, Barnes and Noble, and a festival at Union Square. We organized our own readings at the Brooklyn Moon, Kokobar, and Saata Cafe. On our own, we found out how hard being women could be, but together we discovered the joy, power, and beauty of our womanhood.

The Brooklyn Moon, the offices of *African Voices* magazine, the offices of Harlem River Press, The Nuyorican Poets Cafe, The Afrikan Poetry Theatre, Saata, Borders Books, Tribes Gallery, and Joloff Restaurant were my training grounds. Poetry was everywhere and I was everywhere poetry was. Can you imagine I decided to quit my day job at NBC and devote myself to being a poet?! Like I said, everything seemed possible. jessica Care moore had won the Apollo and started a publishing company; Saul Williams' film *Slam* was a hit at Sundance; Mums was on *Oz*; people were recording CDs like *Eargasm* and *Flippin The Script*; Mike Ladd released *Easy Listening 4 Armageddon;* my friends, The Vibe Chameleons, had toured Europe; The Welfare Poets created uncompromising liberation soundtracks and demanded justice through rhyme; Tony Medina, asha bandele and Suheir Hammad's books had all come out in quick succession. Magic happened every day.

I remember standing in the Brooklyn Moon talking to Tai Allen one evening when a woman he knew walked in. He introduced me to Zoe Anglesey, and once she knew I was a poet, she asked me to fax her work (yes, fax) for a piece she was doing in *Bomb* magazine. The next morning, I faxed the work and the next thing you knew, my work was in *Bomb*. The day I got the magazine I went straight to the Brooklyn Moon. Those of us in the magazine stood around in awe while we scribbled our signatures next to our poems. Later Zoe would edit the anthology *Listen Up!* and include me and eight other poets I respect a great deal. Hey, what wasn't possible?

Back then, Writers and Readers Publishing, Marie Brown and Associates, and *The Quarterly Black Review* were all housed in a little building on Broadway. I think Tony Medina took me over to Writers and Readers for the first time. That office felt sacred. Poets were there working on their first books for the Harlem River Press imprint, and the shelves housed books by authors who had paved the way for us to be the writers we were becoming. I was working on my first manuscript and Deborah Dyson extended the offer to help me edit it. I would go to Writers and Readers and sit with her and we'd look at the poems together.

I went to the office once and got to spend some time with Glenn Thompson, the founder of *Writers and Readers*. He took time to talk to me about running the press, and gave me books by some of the older, established poets he'd published. It was as if he could see the road I was going to walk as a poet and writer, and he wanted to arm me with the words of the women and men who'd moved the stones and cut back the thorny bushes. I think he knew I'd buy all the young poets' books, but with this gesture he was ensuring I'd be fluent in my history. I left that office with six books: Saundra Sharp's *Typing In the Dark*, Safiya Holmes Henderson's *Daily Bread*, Quincy Troupe's *Weather Report*, bell hooks' *A Woman's Mourning Song*, Eugene Redmond's *Eye In The Ceiling*, and Gloria Wade Gayles' *Anointed to Fly*. Glenn and I left the office and walked into the sunny Village afternoon, and I asked him who his favorite poets were. He named Rainer Maria Rilke, William Carlos Williams and someone else—maybe Jorge Luis Borges. I promptly looked into those writers and later bought Rilke's *Letters to a Young Poet*.

I was nurtured and taught by wonderful poets everywhere I went. When I was in undergraduate school in Atlanta I was part of an exciting community of poets as well. Spending time with Jawanza Rand, Kenji Jasper, Gregory Johnson, T'ai Freedom Ford, and Jimmy Woods was a high time. We would read in restaurants, art galleries, dance studios, and occasionally on the Atlanta University Center campuses. Everything was grassroots. Phone calls were made and fliers were printed to get the word out. No one was getting paid. The venues we read at were almost always run by people of color. The poets organized their own events, worked in collectives, and created publications. There was Red Clay, NAPS (Neo-African Poets Society), Oyster Knife, and Cypher. In Atlanta I had a sense that poetry was meant to be a part of a larger conversation. There would be poetry followed by a party, poetry and visual art, poetry and an African dance ensemble, poetry and drumming, poetry in between bands and sometimes poetry and all of the above like at the FunkJazz Kafé. I could also take for granted that the poets around me saw themselves as part of a tradition. We spent a lot of time studying and talking about our favorite writers' work. It was definitely a beautiful time. Those were the '90s.

I never thought that would end, but it did. It took years for me to accept it was over. (Yes, years!) It finally hit me one day when nostalgia led me to go back to the Brooklyn Moon to eat. I went in and people were ordering cocktails and entrees! Back in the poetry days, there were just muffins and tea. I sat back, ordered something and waited for any of my poet friends to show up. None of them did. The neighborhood had changed, there were no poetry readings anymore and I did not know a soul. Our "movement," as I had thought it then, was over. We'd go on to publish, be published, tour the world, do Broadway, become scholars. We'd continue our missions of weaving activism, healing, and words. We'd given each other all we had to offer and then it was time to go in different directions and build in new ways.

What I know is this: it is because of the generosity of the many people I met in the '90s in

New York and Atlanta that I am writing now. Back then, my poet friends and I studied hard, partied hard, loved hard, fought hard, worked hard. We still do actually. Most of us are still friends. I count all those poets, writers, editors, performers, and publishers as part of my family.

Now I can count you as the next generation.

One,
Mariahadessa

Sixteen

Dear Continuum:

Just a quick postcard to remind you that what you are doing is courageous, and that it is a waste of time to compare your work or your process to anyone else's. Your process is your own and it is valid.

I had a colleague who questioned my process and told me about his invisible muse, and how he had to go for days without communicating with others to write a poem. I don't work that way, I told him. In fact, if I needed those conditions to write a poem, no work would ever get done. When I was younger I, like my colleague, believed in the idea of an elusive muse. But now my muse is my mother and my daughters. My muse is my father and my grandparents. My muse is the earth and the homeless man pushing twenty pounds of stuff around in a shopping cart in the snow. My muse is music and love and the dances my husband and I do when the children are asleep. My muse is in my blood. My colleague's way of creating is not the process of a lesser poet or a greater poet, it's simply another process and it reflects another reality. Alice Walker's essay "In Search of Our Mothers' Gardens" keeps coming to mind as I write this. Have you read that yet?

You always have to consider, too, that when people are tearing your process apart, it is usually more about their own frustration than anything remotely connected with you. Consider allowing people into your creative space by invitation only. I hope this is useful to you.

And like my Daddy says, "keep on keepin' on."

One,
Mariahadessa

Seventeen

Dear Continuum:

I hope all is well. Forgive me for taking so long to write you. Between traveling, editing poems, finishing my next book, writing, teaching, being present for my daughters, a lot of things get neglected. I miss staring at the sky, hanging out all night with friends, long phone conversations, dance classes, and painting. I realize that I need to do all those things again. They feed me and my writing.

I did tell you that our very lives are art, and I stand by that, even if I don't always exemplify it. Art goes beyond our pens and paper. Art is our very way of thinking and breathing. I don't have days or weeks of silence, but regular mental rest is critical for me. I go to my favorite restaurant every few weeks to get space to explore, wonder, and just be. Somewhere I read that "we are human beings not human doings." Being can happen in unexpected places like an airport or a crowded subway. It's where I can have access to my own thoughts; it's unhurried space. My art—when it comes from a space of being—is deeper, more complex and layered than that which comes from a whirlwind. Anyway, I can imagine the pressure you feel with your work and the options you're weighing. Things are so different now, and if there weren't others who inhabited that '90s poetry space with me, I'd think I dreamt it all up. Back in the day no one in my circle— or its orbit—ever asked me where I got my MFA. No one. No one asked me what organization or institution I was affiliated with either. When I started sharing my work, poetry was about poetry and community and not about pedigree. I miss that. It felt like every moment was an apprenticeship to word, to color, to struggle, to sound, to movement, to ideas, and to love. I learned to spend more time with elders. Be quiet. Listen. That's where I think this writing thing really starts. Listen. Listen with your entire body and being.

So should you get an MFA or a PhD? Sure, if you want to learn, and certainly if you want to teach. But there are many unemployed and underemployed folks out there with degrees. Nothing is guaranteed.

If you go that route, just remember to keep opening doors for the folks coming behind you. I've seen some people treat poetry as a corporate ladder to climb. I've watched from the sidelines as people climb rungs made up of other poets' backs. There at the top are the prizes, your name in lights, the book deals. I've seen it, and you'll probably see it too. There's a whole lotta inside deals going on too. That is not the only way, but it's the dominant way. You'll know who operates by it. When they realize you can't do anything for them, they back away quickly. Remember, there is another way. It's as ancient as we are. It won't cost you your soul. It won't alienate you from your Grandma. It might even make your work meaningful to her.

I got an MFA from a place no one really knows. I wanted to learn more about writing while being in the Bay Area. I wanted to have more options than I did with a bachelor's degree. I know people are making it work without advanced degrees, but I couldn't. I know some folk who are making it work without any degrees at all. You ask what I'd do? I'd give myself space to decide what is true for me. Everyone's path is different, Continuum. Keep walking yours, and stay connected to your heart.

One,
Mariahadessa

Eighteen

Dear Continuum:

Thank you for sending me a copy of your new chapbook. Congratulations! It is wonderful to see that you and your work keep growing. You asked me what I think about it, but what does it really matter? If I tell you I think your work is fantastic, what will happen? Will the work gain value in your eyes? If I say I don't like it, will it lose its worth? What matters, ultimately, is what you think about your work.

I don't want you to be dependent on anyone's opinions of your work. When you started writing it wasn't to impress me or anyone else. From what you've told me, you started writing to reach people, to shine light into dark closets, to give voice to those who came before you and to those who stand wordless beside you. Has someone come to you after a reading and thanked you for saying what she couldn't? Has a relative called you with tears in his voice and said "What I am wondering is how you know?" Did someone finally write the unsaid thing after a writing circle with you? This is what it seems you are aiming for, not the affirmation of other poets.

With that said, it is critical to work with people who will offer you constructive feedback. This is how we get to be better writers. A fine editor or writing group member knows that the onus is on you to make yourself clear on paper. Their job is to make suggestions to help you strengthen the work. How you employ those suggestions is up to you. At the end of the process it's your truth, your voice that has got to stand up on that page. Remember too that what someone else likes is subjective. Remember that "it is more important to be respected than to be liked." Have you ever heard the saying "what you think about me is none of my business?" What would happen if you applied that idea to your writing life?

Do I care what anyone thinks about my work? Are there people whose respect I would like to earn and keep? Do I listen to constructive criticism? Yes. Yes. And yes. There are a select few people who I talk to about my work before I put it out there. These are people whose missions mirror my own, people whose works, lives, and careers I admire. I've known them all for years and I trust them implicitly. Like I said, this is a small group of people. I also listen to my audiences. They help me know whether my poem is doing what I intended it to do or not. In this way, I am thick-skinned *and* vulnerable. I'm open to criticism in a way that does not stifle me or leave me at someone else's whim.

What will make taking criticism easier—once you've determined who you'll accept it from—is remembering that it is your work being critiqued, not you. Separating your work from yourself helps you not take criticism personally.

And when you offer critique to anyone, offer it with love. Offer it with respect for the person's unique voice and vision.

I hope this is useful.

One,
Mariahadessa

Nineteen

Dear Continuum:

I hope all is well and this message finds you in great health and spirits. Thank you for your careful reading of my poetry. I never know what happens with my work once I let it out in the world. In fact, I don't even think it's much of my business. My job is to do the work, let it go, and create more work. Deeper work at that! But notes like yours are signs that the work is alive and well. Thanks for that.

I've been thinking about your questions about rhythm and the space music can occupy in writing. It would be easier to dance you an answer than grapple with words to articulate one. But I'll try.

Many years ago, I interviewed Kalamu Ya Salaam. I asked him to give me a list of three books he thought no poet could live without. He told me he didn't have such a list. He said, "I often say that in order to get a good grasp of where a person is coming from, I would prefer to see their record collection rather than their books because then I will know for sure what they respond to emotionally as well as intellectually."

His answer shocked me. I always focused on books and reading as a way to become a better writer. But I don't know what sort of writer I'd be without my constant companionship with music. I now know that my voice is probably as influenced by music as it is by books. Studying meter is one thing, being meter is a whole other thing. Being aware of your internal rhythm and the music that exists in most living things can have a profound effect on your work. I'd suggest that whenever you share your work in a reading, lean on your internal music. Give your words permission to shimmy, do the running man, win' or jeté. In fact, attempt to do this on the page, and don't believe that your work is any less literary when you do. Sonia Sanchez has said that the way to edit our work is by reading it aloud. This is not merely a way to scrutinize our word choices; I think this is also a matter of checking the rhythm.

I often say the only artists I envy are musicians. Anyone—no matter what language they speak—can understand music. English has limits. I admire writers who stretch those limits, tease them, or flat-out ignore them. I can't quite say I do that, but much of my writing is inspired by musicians. Some of my work has been carried along by song or created in a church of sound.

You already know that music affects our moods and the way we move. What music do you play on a regular basis? Which artists? What countries do you visit through speakers and headphones? Wouldn't it be great to compare the ways people move to Alice Coltrane with the ways they move to Marvin Gaye? How about Hector Lavoe and Fela? Or Billie Holiday and Buika?

My writing is influenced by all of the arts in which I immerse myself. Music, photography, dance, film, painting, fashion, and sculpture leave their fingerprints on my work and my approaches to creating.

You can walk your way into a poem. In adept hands, words can and do dance. Pianissimo, percussion, and the brass section can be heard in a paragraph. Blues and bops can be written. Study the textures and scents of things. Consider the color of jasmine's scent, the rose's tempo. Let different art forms come into you. They will eventually show up on your pages in surprising ways.

One,
Mariahadessa

P.S.
Get your hands on Ntozake Shange's *Lost in Language and Sound*, Amiri Baraka's *Blues People*, and Stanley Kunitz's essay "The Wisdom of the Body."

Reading List Four

Happy reading!

Marjorie Agosín, *Sargazo=Sargasso: poems*
Amiri Baraka & Paul Vangelisti, *Transbluesency: The Selected Poems of Amiri Baraka/LeRoi Jones (1961-1995)*
Tish Benson, *Wild Like That: Good Stuff Smelling Strong*
LaTasha N. Nevada Diggs, *TwERK*
Henry Dumas, *Knees of a Natural Man*
Lawrence Ferlinghetti, *Poetry as Insurgent Art*
Robert Hass, *The Essential Haiku: Versions of Basho, Buson, and Issa*
Bob Kaufman, *The Ancient Rain: Poems, 1956-1978*
Lauren Muller and The Blueprint Collective, *June Jordan's Poetry for the People: A Revolutionary Blueprint*
Pablo Neruda & Ilan Stevens, *The Poetry of Pablo Neruda*
Mary Oliver, *A Poetry Handbook*
Rainer Maria Rilke, *Letters to a Young Poet*
Askia M. Touré, *From the Pyramids to the Projects: Poems of Genocide and Resistance!*

Essays

Rebirth: What We Don't Say

This story does not have an ending: I am unfolding as a mother, as a writer, as a friend, as a wife, as a daughter and as an individual every moment.

There are things that no woman tells another about motherhood. I will tell you this: I died. It was not childbirth. My labors were long and hard and beautiful. I have given birth twice: once to a screaming soul who shattered my idealistic visions of motherhood, the second time to an infant so ancient she didn't utter a sound as she was lifted by the midwife from the water of the birthing tub. She just stared at us. Both times my heart was cracked—shattered really—and there would be no repairing it. The love that stretched and tore and suckled and broke my sleep was one so profound that nothing could have prepared me for it.

The yellow from the canvas of day bled all over the black watercolor of night and time became nothing. There was a rhythm of waking of feeding and sleeping. Of changing diapers and cuddling and eating again of sleeping again and I was lost in the curves of my children's wrists and in the folds of their necks and the freshly baked bread smell of a new baby and the fragile, startling cries that made me gasp inaudibly and sent my heart flitting in my chest like a desperate butterfly.

Motherhood was all consuming.

There was nothing I wouldn't learn, nothing I wouldn't do to make the journey of my children from the realm of the unknown, the ether, the ancestors, to the harsh world I knew easier. I dove into herbs, homeopathy, and aromatherapy to soothe my first-born, I carried her wrapped around my back in fabric, I was as close to her as her breath. I eliminated all my favorite spices from my diet lest they upset her belly. I devoured writings on mothering. I was too exhausted to write, but I knew that gift was mine and I knew that in time I would get back to it. This gift, this new life, had come through me and it was time to focus on her. I'd get back to me.

When I did get back to me, I was gone. This is the thing that women don't tell each other about motherhood. That you will never be who you were. That you will not see anything the way you used to see it, you will never hear language the way you used to hear it, music, color, photos, friends, family, career path —nothing or no one came through my transition from single woman to mother unexamined. Least of all myself.

I remember walking through the Lower East Side of Manhattan with a friend one evening. My husband pushed our first child down the chilled, narrow sidewalks in a grey stroller while I carried our second baby prominently in my belly. "My whole life had been about me. I was self-centered," I said to our friend. "Of course," my friend replied and he urged me not to feel guilty about that. "This is so different. I am not the center of my universe anymore." It was not guilt I felt. It was as though I was walking between worlds. The old me who roamed the neighborhood we were now in with panther's grace. The me who wound in and out of bookstores and cafes and had nothing but time and her journal on her hands. The me at poetry readings, featured and popular. The me who would disappear for weeks or months, creating at a retreat in Spain or on an adventure in England, sitting rapt in classrooms as teacher or student. That me with her lovers and dramas and poems and phone calls at 3 a.m. And that other me, the one who barely reached for pen and paper. The me who cooked and did laundry and graded papers and shopped for groceries while pushing a stroller. The me with a husband who worked the night shift. I was on, always, no clocking in or out, always breastfeeding, cleaning, changing diapers, singing the alphabet or something. Old friends with self-absorbed ways didn't make sense to me anymore. The city I loved seemed coarse and cold (particularly when no one would give me a seat on the subway.) Who was I then? Full of a quietly growing life, pushing a toddler in a stroller, doing yoga to maintain my equilibrium, living in a tense home, dealing with disappointment at having to do so much alone despite being in a city of millions, some of whom I had called family, some of whom I had called friend.

  I would look in the mirror back then and see a warrior. Glowing skin, quick smile, delicately muscled with tear-stained insides and questions and faith. I did not know that beautiful woman in the mirror. I just knew what she had to do. Knew what she needed to do to help her family get through that day and the next. She was lonely sometimes. I surrendered. Let myself dance invisibly. Let my identity fall through the cracks. Waited for a new self to emerge.

  A new self did emerge. This is what women do not tell each other. I want to say it here: You will die when you become a mother and it will hurt and it will be confusing and you will be someone you never imagined. And then you will be reborn. Truthfully, I have never wanted to be the woman I was before I had children. I loved that woman and I loved that life but I don't want it again. My daughters have made me more daring, more human, more compassionate. Their births have brought me closer to the earth and they have helped me pare my life down to its essentials. Writing, quick prayers, good food, a few close friends, many deep breaths, love, plants, dancing, music, teaching— these are the ingredients of my/this new self. I waited for this new self in the dark, in the bittersweet water of letting go, in the heavy heartbeat of learning to be a mother, against the isolation, I grew and emerged laughing and crying and here I am, sisters and brothers.

Here I am.

The World Is Much Less Safe

If you know where the light is and it goes out it frightens and pours ice through you. Like somehow you got put out in the cold and the darkness. There is no one I fear losing like the poets.
-Amiri Baraka
(from his eulogy for Louis Reyes Rivera)

Dear Amiri Baraka:

You told me not to work too hard. And because you were here, I didn't have to. Now *you split*. And *the world is less safe*. So me and Jessica and Tony and asha and Thomas and Ahi and Bonafide and Willie and Dominique—all of your children, blood and not, find ourselves working double time. Triple time trying to do what you made look so easy.

You said *nothing dies but that which never lived*. And so you are live as live can be and always will be

but damn

we miss you.

One,
Mariahadessa

***

January 7, 2014 was one of the coldest days on record in New York City. I had to go out. I was the only person in my house who wasn't laid out with the flu and I was trying my best to take care of everyone. Chicken soup, I told myself. Chicken soup will take

care of everything. I bundled up and went outside.
-carrots
-oregano
-celery
-chicken breasts
-wide egg noodles
-chicken stock (I didn't have all day to make stock)

I got home, started the soup and received a message that said that Amiri Baraka was being given days to live. I finished the soup, put it in bowls, ate and then I got into bed with fever, pain in my head, my ears, my wrists, my hips, my left breast too. My husband will tell you that I moaned, "I'm going to die" over and over.

I did not get back up for four days. From my bed I called the poets I knew who loved Amiri Baraka. No one knew what to say. I was coughing and feverish. Some of my friends made me laugh by reminding me of funny things Mr. Baraka had done or said. Fuck what you heard, Amiri Baraka was hilarious.

Kanye West's next big hit/ needs to be upside his head!-A.B.

If Elvis Presley/ is
        King
Who is James Brown,
        GOD?-A.B.

"Remember the party where the Barakas were beating the metal chairs?"
"Yeah."

When I was in Albany, Georgia with Amiri Baraka, Thomas Sayers Ellis and Pearl Cleage for the

Transcendence Poetry Festival, there were times I had to make sure I didn't choke on my shrimp and grits I was laughing so hard. Thomas and Baraka kept me, Ahi, and the festival staff in stitches. Between stories about the sixties, Smokey Robinson concerts and a little talk about poetry (*These people write like there never was a struggle*-A.B.), we were raucous with joy.

I never imagined that two months later I'd be in Newark at Mr. Baraka's wake and funeral. Be at his house, which was full of folks, where Baraka seemed to look at us from a large photograph.

He was and he wasn't all at once. We were and we weren't all at once.

How can I explain what Amiri Baraka meant to my generation of poets? We who call ourselves children of the Black Arts Movement? We feminist, activist, writing-for-justice poets?

Baraka was there. More than there. He was available and deeply present. He was as committed to us as he was to his craft. Baraka built institutions, created safe spaces where we could share our work, called out those folks who didn't have our best interests at heart, he lived in the Black community and organized. He could have just published his books and created a comfortable life for himself, but he was too dedicated to truth to do that. He was too dedicated to us to do that.

Last year when Amiri Baraka saw that many of my peers—such as jessica Care moore and Saul Williams —were left out of an anthology on Black poetry, he challenged the editor publicly on it. Baraka was in the anthology but he championed our work. He paid attention. He took us seriously. He loved us and he made it plain. He ain't give a damn about where we got our degrees or if we even had them. He wanted us to contribute to our communities and make art that is useful. That's why his death cuts so deep. That's why we're scarred. That is why we work so damn hard.

***

During my almost twenty years of sharing poetry I'd encountered Mr. Baraka a number of times. Each time was special in its own way.

The first was in '95 as an undergraduate student at Clark Atlanta University. "Baraka is going to say something to cause trouble," my friend Seitu said with twinkling eyes. Of course we were at that 2 p.m. program with bells on. I'm sure Mr. Baraka called somebody out, but what I remember was crowding around him after he had spoken. I think this was when he gave out copies of his speeches on "Revolutionary Art."

In July 1996 my work with African Voices literary journal would land me in the Barakas' basement reading poetry at "Kimako's Blues People." Then I saw the Barakas partied as hard as they organized and wrote. The reading, live music and joyous shouts were still going on when we left the house at about 2 a.m. I bought a copy of the chapbook *Bop Trees* and after he signed it, I looked at the inscription again and again: "unity and struggle," he'd written as he often did. He told me poets should not be afraid to publish their own work. Eventually, I would take his advice and create two chapbooks.

My involvement with Felipe Luciano's Wordchestra, which Tony Medina used to jokingly call the "We Are The World of poetry," meant that I also rehearsed with Amina and Amiri Baraka practically every week for a few months as part of a poetry chorus. We young poets knew we'd hit the jackpot! We practiced poems every week with folks like Louis Reyes Rivera, Sandra Maria Esteves, Pedro Pietri, Safiya Henderson-Holmes, and the Barakas. The poems had been broken up into main parts, read by the author, and lines that we'd say as a group. I most remember practicing Louis Reyes Rivera's "Bullet Cry," Halim Suliman's "Couldn't Stop Bebop," and Amina Baraka's "Slave Legacy." My shyness often got the best of me in that environment and I'd simply do the work and observe people.

Years would pass before I'd see Amiri Baraka again. I'd had children, lived on two other continents, left the stage and poetry, and returned to it. It was 2012. Mr. Baraka was reading a eulogy at the funeral of his close friend Louis Reyes Rivera. Baraka's words stirred me on a deeper level than they had when I was younger. It was hard to stop my tears.

The next time I saw Mr. Baraka was March 2013 at the Afrikan Poetry Theatre. I had the fortune of being one of four poets who opened his program. Talk about nervous. It had been years since I'd interacted with him and I knew he would not remember me, but I hoped he'd see I was trying to carry on the work he did. When I read my poem

75

"Forced Entry," which is about date rape, I introduced the piece by thanking him for his work and saying, "Amiri Baraka taught us that we have to use our words to help fight all the wars being waged against us." After the reading, Mr. Baraka studied me and said *That was a strong poem.*

And you wanna ask me if the man was sexist? Homophobic? Please go read a book. Try one after the 1970s. Don't you see all the transformation, self-reflection and struggle on those pages?

***

You have to criticize yourself for the errors you've made because that's the only way you can break with them.

My wife, Amina, waged a constant struggle against my personal and organizational male chauvinism.

All the black women in those militant black organizations deserve the highest praise. Not only did they stand with us shoulder to shoulder against black people's enemies, they also had to go toe to toe with us, battling day after day against our insufferable male chauvinism.

Read Amiri Baraka's devastating piece about his daughter Shani Baraka's murder. He names the sickness that killed his child: homophobia and woman hating.

***

Most people never examine the ways they oppress others, but Amiri Baraka dared to check himself again and again and he did it in public!

Take a glance at Baraka's comrades, friends, the artists he supported and mentored and inspired. Look at them. They are gay and straight and women and men and they are from all over the globe.

(Is it just easier to say the man was anti something? He was love and pro us, so ever evolving, so fierce in protecting us and resisting everything bent on our deaths. Is it easier to freeze him in earlier positions that even he had moved far from because he was more dangerous when he loved us ALL?)

(Oh you want to write lies about Baraka? I hope your pens explode, I hope your computers regurgitate, I hope your administrative assistants go on strike, and your email accounts get hacked, and your tenure tracks derail.)

(And while I'm at it, American poetry is just a mirror of America itself: segregated, classist, run by a network of good ol' boys who shut out voices like mine by pretending that we don't exist. Being spiritual kin to Zora and Langston and Baraka means speaking anyway and taking pride in the poetry communities that raised and continue to nurture me. I'm steeped in the life-affirming brews my cultural working comrades write and be. I had no idea anyone could react with anything but grief at news of Baraka's death. There were grumblings about the obituaries written in large publications, but my center of gravity is such that I read those with handfuls of salt. [What Fanon termed "combat breathing" becomes second nature in an occupied literary territory, you know?])

Meanwhile people everywhere know where Baraka stands. That is why we came from all over to mourn and celebrate on January 17th and 18th. That's why there are tributes to him across the globe. That's why riding the packed bus to the wake I heard a teenager say softly, "That's where they are having the wake for Baraka" and the sounds of drums filled the air. That's why the community of Newark came out en masse. Did you hear the fire department play their bagpipes at the funeral? Person after person stood up in the church at the wake and testified—yes, testified—about who Amiri Baraka was and how he had changed them, supported them, loved them.

What I'll remember most was probably eating breakfast with Mr. Baraka on the last morning of the festival. He was concerned that his son Ahi wouldn't have time to eat breakfast. And when I told him that I had to pack and get ready for my reading and Thomas rushed into the dining room scrambling to get breakfast before his workshop, Mr. Baraka, who was packed and ready for a flight that would not be leaving for hours, said *you young people always wait until the last minute*. (To this day, when I am rushing around in a hotel room trying to get ready for a reading, I hear Mr. Baraka saying this.)

I'll remember that he talked to us the night before about the murders of his sister Kimako and his daughter Shani. *You women have it tough* he said. His face held an expression I had not seen over the years I'd encountered him. Devastation lay heavy in his voice. We talked about sexual assault and violence against women. That was the only time I'd seen Mr. Baraka look puzzled. He loved all of us. I can tell you that.

I was just getting to know the man. I'm going to miss him. That's what I'm saying. That's all I'm saying. And when I said good-bye to Amiri Baraka and hugged him in Georgia, for some reason, I decided to turn back around and hug him again. "Just one more," I said.

***

With the deaths of great poets like Jayne Cortez, Sekou Sundiata, Louis Reyes Rivera the world is much less safe.
                                                                    -Amiri Baraka

Notes

Names from Letter One:

Langston Hughes, James Baldwin,
Zora Neale Hurston, Alice Walker,
Margaret Walker, Frank X Walker,
Ntozake Shange, Amiri Baraka,
Amina Baraka, Robert Hayden,
Henry Dumas, asha bandele,
Jacqueline Johnson, Aracelis Girmay,
jessica Care moore, Carl Hancock Rux,
Suheir Hammad, Adrienne Rich,
Lucille Clifton, Cheryl Boyce-Taylor,
Tony Medina, Gwendolyn Brooks,
Haki Madhubuti, Carolyn Forche,
Kalamu Ya Salaam, Bonafide Rojas,
Luis Reyes Rivera, Etheridge Knight,
Sandra Maria Esteves, Layding Kaliba,
Shariff Simmons, Danny Simmons,
Bob Kaufman, Sonia Sanchez,
Nikky Finney, Tara Betts,
Martin Espada, & Willie Perdomo.

A Few More Ideas

Literary Journals

This is a short list of literary journals to help give you an idea of the range of some of the writing being published. I've had work published in some of them. Most of these publications are open to emerging voices and/or have a tradition of publishing work by socially engaged writers:

African-American Review
African Voices Magazine
Acentos Review
Blackberry
Black Renaissance Noire
Callaloo
Crab Orchard Review
Drunken Boat
Kweli
Mosaic
North American Review
Obsidian
Pierian
Pluck!
Rattle
The Missouri Review
Tin House
This

Conferences

The first three conferences I've listed place emphasis on activism and art. Furious Flower only happens once every ten years! I've included AWP because its annual conference is a huge gathering of writers from all over the globe:

Split This Rock
National Black Writers Conference
Furious Flower
Association Of Writers & Writing Programs (AWP)

References

Baldwin, James. "Sonny's Blues." *Going To Meet The Man.* New York: Vintage International, 1995. 101-141. Print.

Forman, Ruth. "Poetry Should Ride the Bus." *We Are the Young Magicians.* Boston: Beacon Press, 1993. Print.

Lorde, Audre. "The Transformation of Silence into Language and Action." *Sister Outsider: Essays and Speeches.* New York, The Crossing Press, 1984. Print

Madhubuti, Haki. *Run Toward Fear: New Poems and a Poet's Handbook.* Chicago: Third World Press, 2004. Print.

Shange, Ntozake. "Inquiry." *Nappy Edges.* New York: St Martin's Press, 1972. Print.

Gratitude

Spirit first always.

Dominique, I'm convinced that nobody loves as deeply as you do. You are earth, mountain, & the ability to move mountains. I love you. Mariette Thoonen who creates space for work & play. John & Jewell Tallie who came to countless readings and believed that their child had & has something to say. Serene & Joy-Shanti, you make me fight harder, dig deeper, & love in ways that seemed impossible.

Big up to Rosebud Ben-Oni for championing and publishing the first letter. Shout-out to Thomas Sayers Ellis for gentle feedback that alchemized "The World is Much Less Safe."

This book has been a journey & a small, very committed cadre of folks helped me get through it.

Gratitude to: Timothy Prolific Jones, your wonderful spirit & thoughtful comments inspired more letters and let me know this book was needed. Shauna Morgan Kirlew, your eagle eyes, sage spirit, nurture & humor transformed this work. I'm forever grateful. Frank X Walker, without you this book would still be a Google doc & we'd be crowdfunding. Your unshakeable belief in these letters & the urgency of this work kept me going even more than the bourbon did! Asante sana & Modupe, Brother. My beautiful family at The Watering Hole, you resuscitated something necessary in my soul. Crystal Clarity, you & your work are the purest magic. Jeff Mack, thank you for believing in what I can do even when I'm in doubt.

Bonafide, look at you publishing people! Yes. We did it! Patricia Milanes, I knew I could exhale when you stepped in. Big-up to Mirlande Jean-Gilles, Carolyn Butts, Tony Medina, Cheryl Boyce-Taylor, Willie Perdomo, Kalamu Ya Salaam, & Jacqueline Johnson for moral support during the writing process. Sometimes the words "Go 'head" were all I needed to hear. Y'all said it.

Biography

Mariahadessa Ekere Tallie is the author of *Karma's Footsteps* (Flipped Eye). She is the Poetry Editor of the literary magazine *African Voices*. Her work has been published in *North American Review*, *WSQ: Women's Studies Quarterly*, *Black Renaissance Noire*, *VIDA*, *Crab Orchard Review*, and *BOMB*. Tallie's work is the subject of the short film, "I Leave My Colors Everywhere." She is the recipient of a 2010 Queens Council on the Arts grant for her research on herbalists of the African diaspora. Tallie earned an MFA from Mills College in 2002. She has taught literature and composition at York College and Medgar Evers College in New York City. Her children, the young people she meets when she travels, and justice are her biggest inspirations.

www.ekeretallie.com

Made in the USA
Las Vegas, NV
14 January 2021

15847909R10059